Unleashing Your Inner Brand

Personal Branding for a Purposeful Life

MUSTAFA SHAKEEL SHAIKH

© 2024 Mustafa Shaikh

All rights reserved.
No part of this publication may be reproduced, distributed, or transmitted in any form or by any means, including photocopying, recording, or other electronic or mechanical methods, without the prior written permission of the author, except for brief quotations in a review or critical article, as permitted by copyright law.

Disclaimer: This ebook is a work of fiction/non-fiction. Names, characters, businesses, places, events, and incidents are either products of the author's imagination or used in a fictitious manner. Any resemblance to actual persons, living or dead, or actual events is purely coincidental. For permissions or inquiries, please

For permissions or inquiries, please contact:
Mustafa Shaikh
(work) mustafa@brandliftz.com
(personal) i.msshk2002@gmail.com

For those who dare to live their truth and share it with the world. You are the authors of your story.

Acknowledgments

Writing this book has been a journey filled with growth, reflection, and collaboration. I'd like to thank my family for their unwavering support and belief in me. To my mentors and colleagues, your guidance has helped shape this book into what it is today. Finally, to my readers—thank you for embarking on this journey with me. May your personal brand inspire the world as much as it inspires you.

"Your brand is a story unfolding across all customer touch points." — Jonah Sachs

Table of Contents

Chapter 1: The Essence of Personal Branding
Chapter 2: Discovering Your Core Values
Chapter 3: Defining Your Purpose
Chapter 4: Crafting Your Unique Brand Identity
Chapter 5: The Power of Authentic Storytelling
Chapter 6: Communicating Your Brand to the World
Chapter 7: Evolving and Sustaining Your Brand
Conclusion
Epilogue
About the Author

Introduction
THE BEGINNING OF YOUR JOURNEY

Welcome to the adventure of discovering your personal brand! In today's world, being true to yourself and showing up authentically has never been more important. The world is waiting for the unique story only you can tell. But personal branding isn't just about self-promotion—it's about purpose, vision, and living your truth.

Imagine this: you're walking down a path. It's a little foggy, and while you're not sure what's ahead, you know this path leads to the future you desire. This path is your personal brand—how you live your values, how you communicate your vision, and how you leave a lasting impact on others. Unleashing Your Inner Brand is your guide to navigating this path with confidence, intention, and purpose.

Get ready to embark on a journey of self-discovery. By the end, you'll not only understand what your personal brand is, but you'll also feel empowered to live it authentically. Let's take that first step together.

Chapter 1: The Essence of Personal Branding

What if your story was your most powerful tool?

Personal branding is about defining the narrative that speaks to who you are at your core. It's how the world perceives you, and more importantly, how you present yourself to the world. Think of a book—the cover, the title, the introduction—they all tell part of the story. But the real essence lies within the pages, the details, and the message you convey. Your personal brand is no different.

Consider the story of Steve Jobs. His personal brand wasn't built overnight. It came from a lifetime of innovation, vision, and, yes, failure. But each part of his journey, every success and setback, shaped his personal brand. The same is true for you. Your story has already begun; now it's time to shape how it's told.

Your personal brand is the narrative that captures your values, passions, and skills in a way that feels authentically you. The question is, how will you tell your story?

Chapter 2: Discovering Your Core Values

Your values are the compass that guide your journey.

In life, we all face moments of uncertainty. These are the times when our core values become our guiding light. They are the principles that keep us grounded and true to ourselves. Whether it's integrity, creativity, or perseverance, your values are the foundation of your personal brand.

Let's reflect on Malala Yousafzai's story. She stood up for education and equality in the face of overwhelming adversity. Her unwavering commitment to her values made her a global symbol of courage. Now, think about your own life. What moments have defined you? What values do you stand for, no matter the circumstance?

Identifying your values is the first step in building a brand that feels authentic. Once you've discovered what truly matters to you, you can begin living and sharing your values with the world.

Chapter 3: Defining Your Purpose

What drives you?

Purpose is the fire in your soul. It's the reason you get up in the morning, and the fuel that keeps you going when things get tough. Defining your purpose is a powerful act of self-discovery, and it's central to your personal brand. Without purpose, your brand can feel hollow—like a beautiful house with no foundation.

Take Oprah Winfrey as an example. Her purpose has always been clear: to inspire and uplift others. Everything she does, from her talk show to her philanthropic work, reflects that core purpose. And because she's so deeply aligned with her "why," her personal brand is not only strong—it's transformational.

Now, it's time to define your purpose. Ask yourself: What impact do you want to make on the world? How do you want to be remembered? Write it down. Refine it. And let it guide your brand, every step of the way.

Chapter 4: Crafting Your Unique Brand Identity

No one else can be you. That is your superpower.

Your brand identity is how you bring your values and purpose to life. It's not just the words you say, but how you say them. It's the visuals you choose, the tone of your voice, and the experiences you create for others. Think of it as the storybook of your brand—every page, every detail contributes to the bigger picture.

Jeff Bezos, the founder of Amazon, built his brand on innovation, customer obsession, and long-term thinking. His brand identity is synonymous with his commitment to pushing boundaries and thinking ahead. What words describe your brand? Are you bold, empathetic, or perhaps visionary?

Your brand identity is how the world sees you, so make sure it's true to who you are. This is your story—write it your way.

Chapter 5: The Power of Authentic Storytelling

People don't connect with perfection—they connect with authenticity.

Stories have been the most powerful way to connect with others since the beginning of time. We don't remember every detail about people we meet, but we remember how they made us feel, and stories have the power to create emotional connections. Your brand story is no different.

Look at brands like Nike, which tells stories of perseverance and victory through their "Just Do It" campaign. They don't just sell shoes; they sell a belief in human potential. That's the power of a story well-told.

Now, think about your story. What challenges have shaped you? What victories have defined your journey? When you tell your story authentically, you create a brand that resonates on a deeper level. Don't be afraid to share the highs and the lows—because they are what make you, you.

Chapter 6: Communicating Your Brand to the World

Your voice matters.

It's not enough to have a brand—you need to share it. And the way you communicate your brand can make all the difference. In today's digital world, there are endless platforms and opportunities to connect with your audience. But it's not about being everywhere; it's about being intentional and authentic in your communication.

Take Gary Vaynerchuk, a master of brand communication. He uses social media to share his message of hustle, gratitude, and self-awareness, building a global following. He doesn't just talk at people; he engages with them.

What platforms will you use to share your brand? Whether it's Instagram, LinkedIn, or a personal blog, choose the ones that align with your message. And remember, communication is a two-way street. Engage with your audience, listen to their feedback, and be open to growth.

Chapter 7: Evolving and Sustaining Your Brand

Your brand is a journey, not a destination.

Like you, your brand will evolve over time. The person you are today may not be the same person you'll be in five or ten years, and that's okay. In fact, it's necessary. Your brand should grow and evolve with you, reflecting the lessons you learn and the experiences you have along the way.

Take Madonna, the Queen of Reinvention. Throughout her career, she's evolved her brand again and again, staying relevant by embracing change. She never shied away from evolution, and neither should you.

Make it a habit to check in with your brand regularly. Ask yourself: Does my brand still reflect who I am? Does it align with my values and purpose? If not, it's time for a refresh. Remember, growth is not only natural—it's essential.

Conclusion

Your Brand, Your Story

Congratulations! You've embarked on a journey to discover your personal brand, and that journey will continue for a lifetime. You've learned to define your values, uncover your purpose, and craft a brand that feels authentically you. But this is just the beginning.

Your brand is your legacy. It's the story of who you are and the impact you want to leave on the world. So, continue to live your truth, tell your story, and inspire others with your authenticity.

Epilogue

Keep Telling Your Story

The path to unleashing your inner brand is ongoing. Just like life, your personal brand is not static—it's dynamic, ever-changing, and deeply personal. As you move forward, embrace the challenges and celebrate the victories. Each moment is another chapter in your brand story.

The world needs your story—so keep telling it, keep living it, and keep believing in the unique power that only you possess. Your journey is far from over, and the best is yet to come.

About the Author

BEGINNING OF YOUR JOURNEY

Mustafa Shaikh is an accomplished personal branding consultant, digital strategist, and eBook publishing expert with a passion for helping individuals and businesses define their unique identities. Over the years, Mustafa has guided countless entrepreneurs, leaders, and creatives on their journeys to build powerful personal brands rooted in authenticity and purpose. His work blends storytelling with practical strategies, empowering people to unleash their inner potential.

When he's not helping others build their brands, Mustafa enjoys reading, writing, and continually exploring the ever-changing landscape of digital marketing and personal development.

You can connect with Mustafa With email:

(work) mustafa@brandliftz.com

(personal) i.msshk2002@gmail.com

Appendices

Core Values Discovery Worksheet

Your core values shape your decisions, actions, and interactions. This worksheet will help you uncover and prioritize your personal values to build a brand rooted in authenticity.

1. List 10 Values That Resonate With You
   (Examples: Integrity, Creativity, Leadership, Empathy, Innovation)
   1. _____
   2. _____
   3. _____
   4. _____
   5. _____
   6. _____
   7. _____
   8. _____
   9. _____

10. _____
___

2. Rank Them In Order of Importance

Reflect on the values that guide your life and brand. Rank them from most to least important:

1. _____
   ___
2. _____
   ___
3. _____
   ___
4. _____
   ___
5. _____
   ___

3. REFLECTION QUESTIONS

a) How do these values show up in your daily life?
b) In what ways do you want to align your actions more closely with these values?

Unique Value Proposition (UVP) Template

Your Unique Value Proposition (UVP) is what sets you apart. This template will guide you through crafting a UVP that highlights your strengths and communicates the value you bring to others.

1. Identify Your Strengths

List your top three skills or talents that define your work or approach:

1. _____
   ___
2. _____
   ___
3. _____
   ___

2. Understand Your Audience

Who do you want to reach with your personal brand? What are their needs and desires?

1. Audience: _____
2. Their Needs: _____
3. How Can You Help? _____

3. Craft Your UVP Statement

Combine your strengths and audience needs into a one-sentence statement that highlights your unique value:

    a) "I help [audience] achieve [result] by [how you help]."

Brand Storytelling Framework

Stories make your brand memorable. Use this framework to structure a compelling personal brand story.

1. Setting
Where did your journey begin? What inspired you to start building your personal brand?

2. Conflict

What challenges or obstacles have you faced on your journey?

3. **Resolution**
   How did you overcome those challenges? What successes or turning points have shaped your brand?
4. **Message**
   What is the key takeaway you want people to remember about your story?

Brand Storytelling Framework

Stories make your brand memorable. Use this framework to structure a compelling personal brand story.

1) **Setting**
   Where did your journey begin? What inspired you to start building your personal brand?
2) **Conflict**
   What challenges or obstacles have you faced on your journey?
3) **Resolution**
   How did you overcome those challenges? What successes or turning points have shaped your brand?
4) **Message**
   What is the key takeaway you want people to remember about your story?

Social Media Content Planner

Consistency in sharing your personal brand on social media is key. This planner will help you map out content that aligns with your brand identity.

1. Identify Your Platforms
   (Examples: Instagram, LinkedIn, Twitter)
   - Platform 1: _____
   - Platform 2: _____
   - Platform 3: _____

2. Content Ideas

List 5 content ideas that align with your brand message:

1. _____
   _
2. _____
   _
3. _____
   _
4. _____
   _
5. _____
   _

3. Call to Action

What action do you want your audience to take after engaging with your content?
   - Example: Sign up for my newsletter, download my free guide, etc.

Weekly Reflection Journal

To stay aligned with your brand, regular reflection is important. Use these weekly prompts to track your progress and keep your brand on course.

1. What actions did you take this week that aligned with your core values?

_____
_____

2. What challenges did you face in staying authentic?

_____
_____

3. How will you adjust or evolve your brand moving forward?

_____
_____

2. Content Ideas

List 5 content ideas that align with your brand message:

1. _____
   -
2. _____
   -
3. _____
   -
4. _____
   -
5. _____
   -

3. Call to Action

What action do you want your audience to take after engaging with your content?

- Example: Sign up for my newsletter, download my free guide, etc.

Thank You

As I bring this journey to a close, I want to take a moment to thank you—the reader. Writing this book has been a deeply personal and fulfilling experience, but it wouldn't mean much without people like you who seek to discover and express their true selves.

Thank you for trusting me to guide you on your path to unleashing your inner brand. My hope is that the insights and exercises within these pages have inspired you to think deeply, reflect authentically, and act courageously. Your personal brand is one of your most powerful tools, and I am honored to be a part of your journey to embrace it fully.

Remember, your story matters. You have the power to impact the world in ways you may never have imagined. Keep growing, keep evolving, and most importantly—keep being you.

With gratitude,

Mustafa Shaikh

Inspirational Quotes

"The only way to do great work is to love what you do."
— **Steve Jobs**

"Success is liking yourself, liking what you do, and liking how you do it." — **Maya Angelou**

"Your personal brand is a promise to your clients... a promise of quality, consistency, competency, and reliability."
— **Jason Hartman**

"The best way to predict the future is to create it."
— **Peter Drucker**

"Don't be afraid to give up the good to go for the great."
— **John D. Rockefeller**

"Your brand is the single most important investment you can make in your business." — **Steve Forbes**

A Personal Note to You

As you turn the final pages of this book, I encourage you to reflect on everything you've learned. But don't stop here. Personal branding is a journey that evolves with every step you take, every decision you make, and every connection you build. This book is a guide, but the true work begins with you.

Take what resonates with you from these chapters, apply it to your life, and watch how your personal brand unfolds. You are the author of your own story, and the world is waiting to hear your voice.

Thank you for being part of this experience. If you found this book helpful, I would be deeply grateful if you could share it with others. Your recommendations, reviews, and feedback help to spread the message of living authentically and purposefully.

Finally, always remember: You are enough. Your brand is already inside of you, waiting to be unleashed. Go forth boldly and tell your story.

With warmest regards,

Mustafa Shaikh

MUSTAFA SHAKEEL SHAIKH

YOU CAN CONNECT WITH MUSTAFA WITH EMAIL:
(WORK) MUSTAFA@BRANDLIFTZ.COM
(PERSONAL) I.MSSHK2002@GMAIL.COM

www.ingramcontent.com/pod-product-compliance
Lightning Source LLC
Chambersburg PA
CBHW040330220526
45473CB00009B/2629